I0473012

Unicorns & Pixie Dust

A Dreamer's Coloring Book
by Brandy Woods

www.brandywoods.com
spiritart.brandywoods.com

Copyright © 2015 Brandy Woods
ISBN 978-0-9938326-4-2

All rights reserved. No part of this book may be used or reproduced in any manner whatsoever without written permission. Coloring pages are for personal use only. For more information, address the author.

Second CreateSpace edition
First printing via Lulu: December 2015

Printed in the USA

10 9 8 7 6 5 4 3 2

If you purchased this book without a cover, you should be aware that this book is stolen property. It was reported as "unsold and destroyed" to the publisher, and neither the author nor the publisher has received any payment for this "stripped book."

"To be yourself in a world that is constantly trying to make you something else is the greatest accomplishment." ~ *Ralph Waldo Emerson*

I would like to dedicate this book to anyone who ever believed in faeries or unicorns, and to anyone who needs a little extra magic in their life!

Always trust your heart and your dreams, and magic will follow!

~Brandy Woods, December 2015

I, _____, hereby promise to be true to myself, and love myself no matter what.

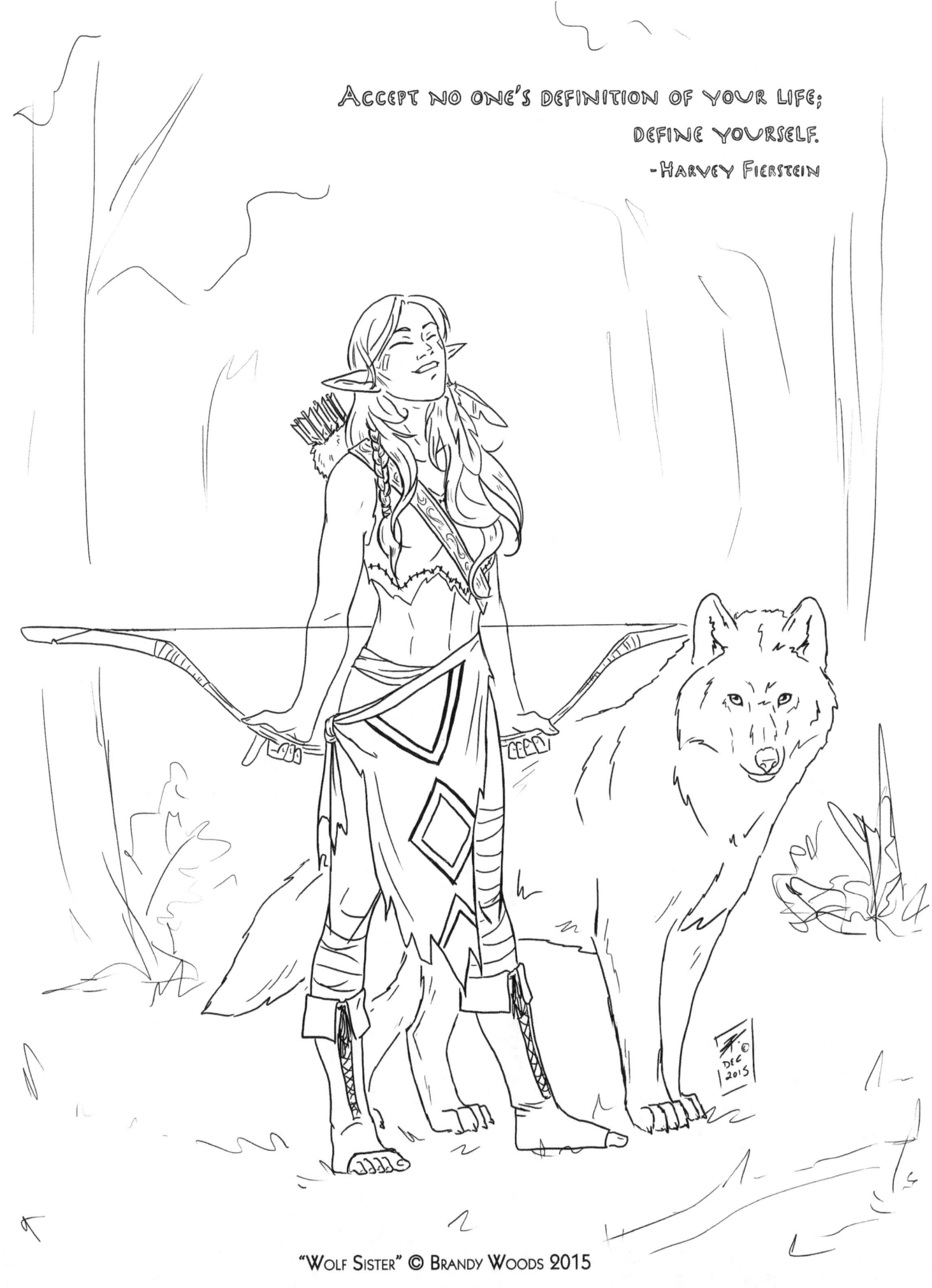

ACCEPT NO ONE'S DEFINITION OF YOUR LIFE;
DEFINE YOURSELF.
-HARVEY FIERSTEIN

"WOLF SISTER" © BRANDY WOODS 2015

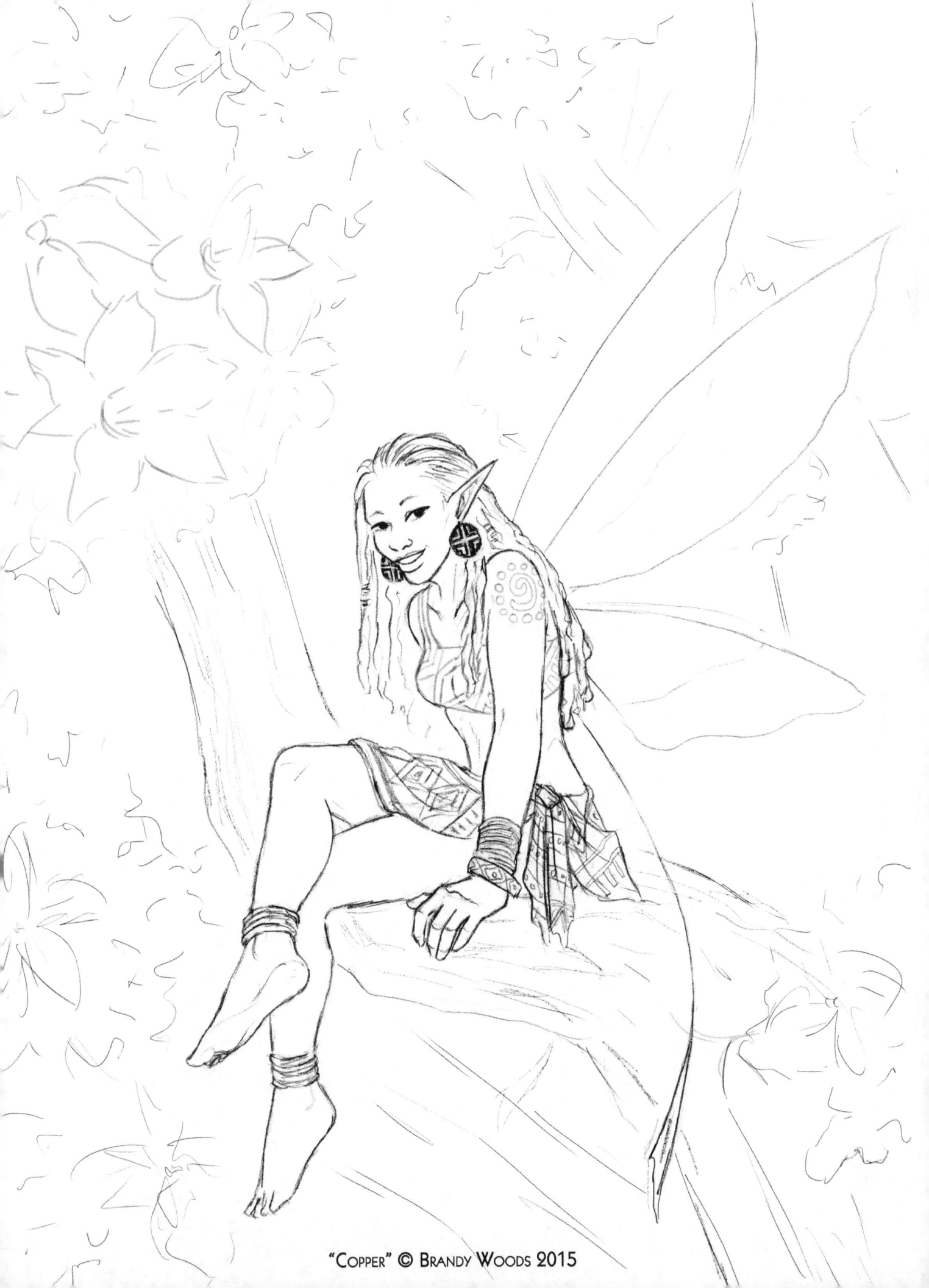

"Copper" © Brandy Woods 2015

BE YOURSELF: EVERYONE ELSE IS ALREADY TAKEN.
- OSCAR WILDE

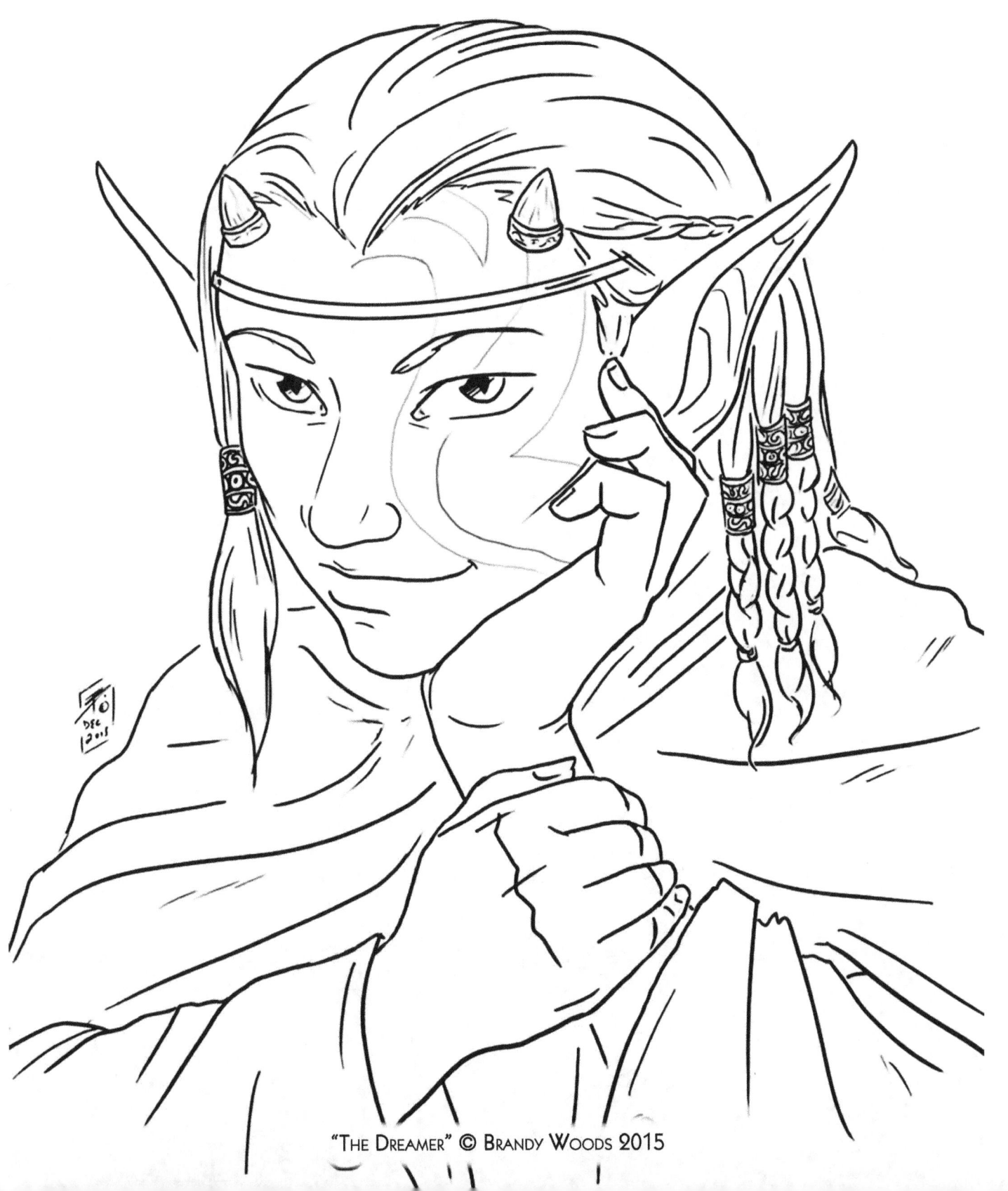

"The Dreamer" © Brandy Woods 2015

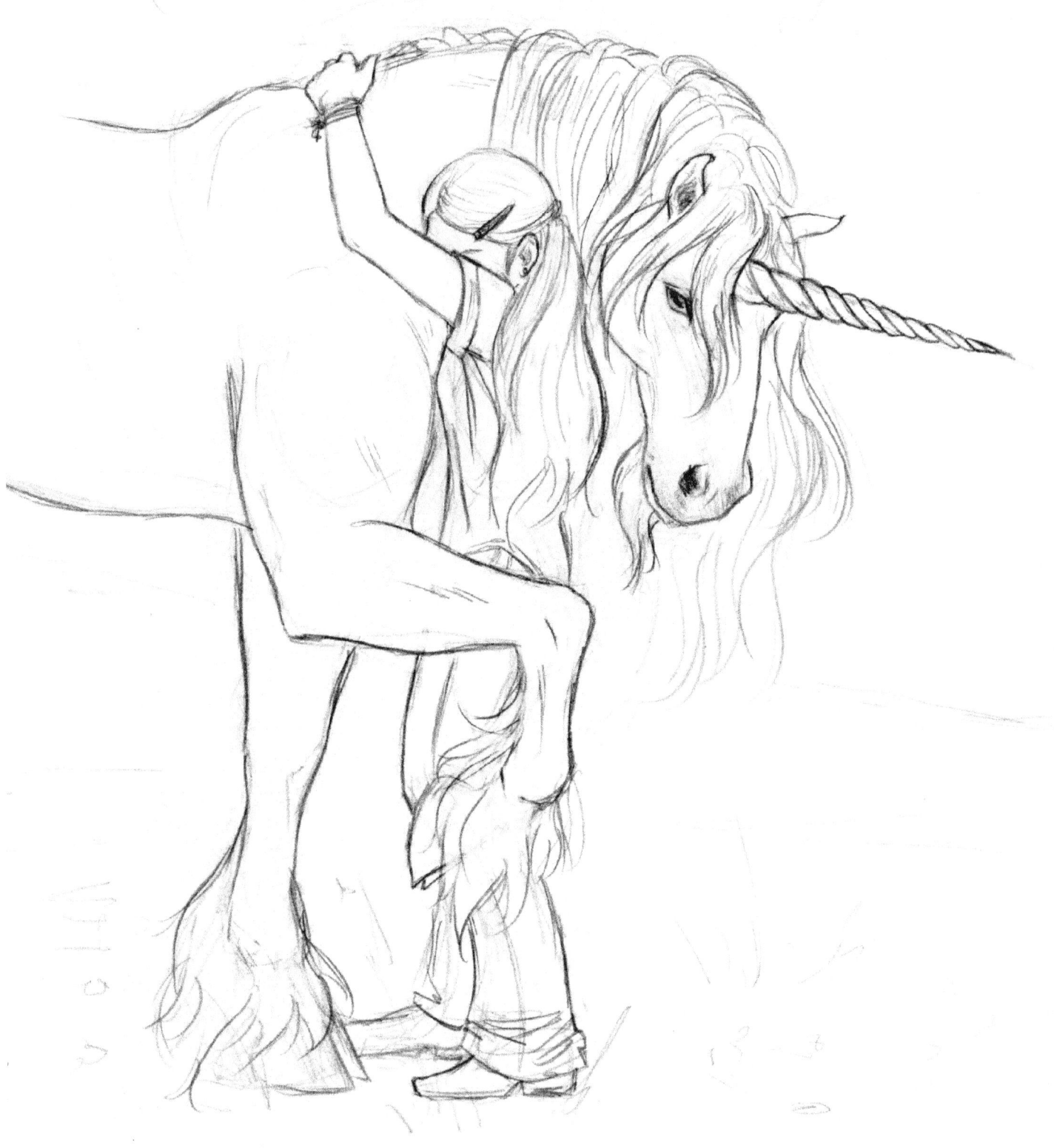

"CHLOE AND THE UNICORN" © BRANDY WOODS 2015

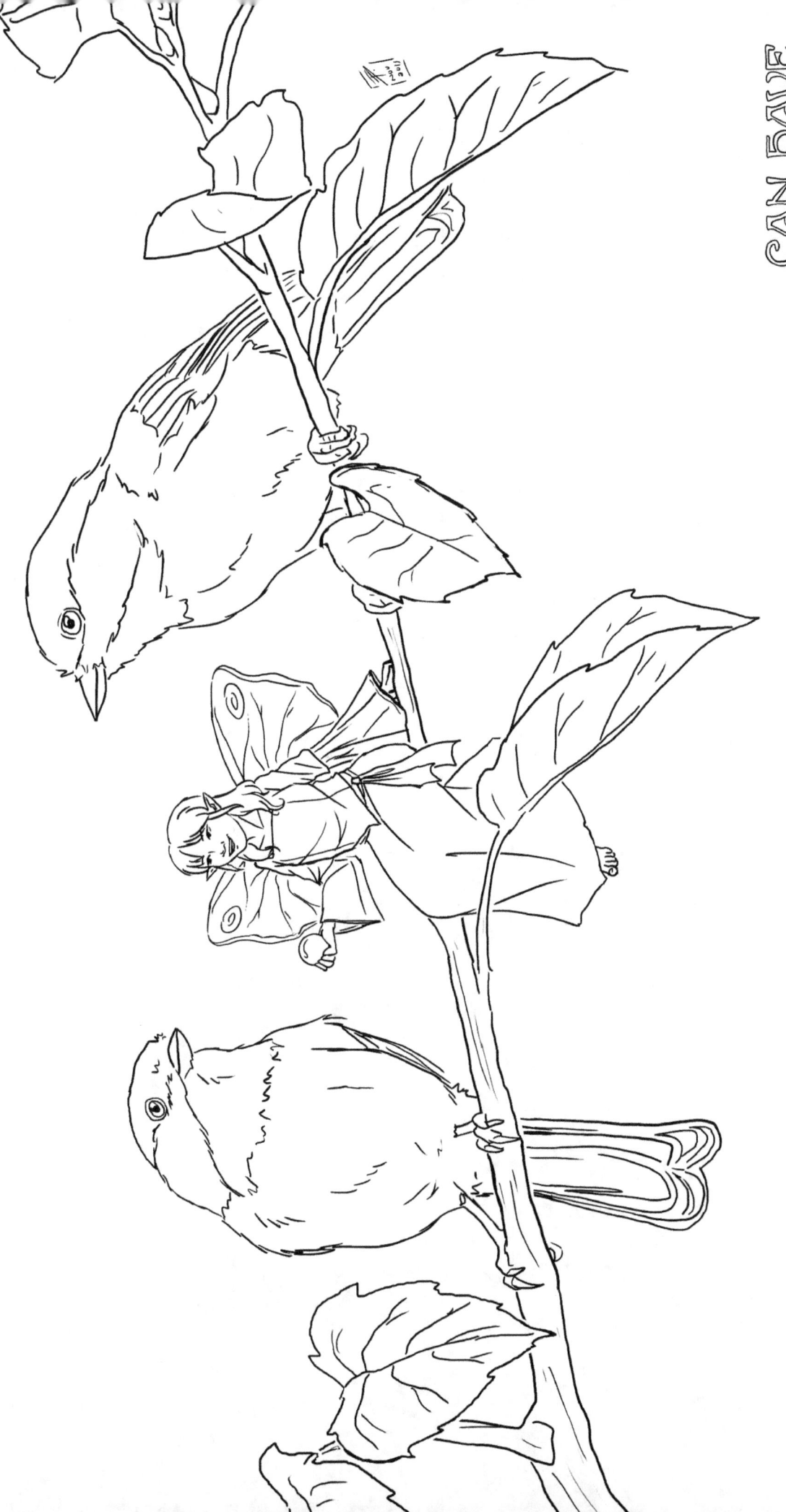

EVEN THE SMALLEST VOICE...

...CAN HAVE

SOMETHING BIG TO SAY

"Harmony" © Brandy Woods 2015

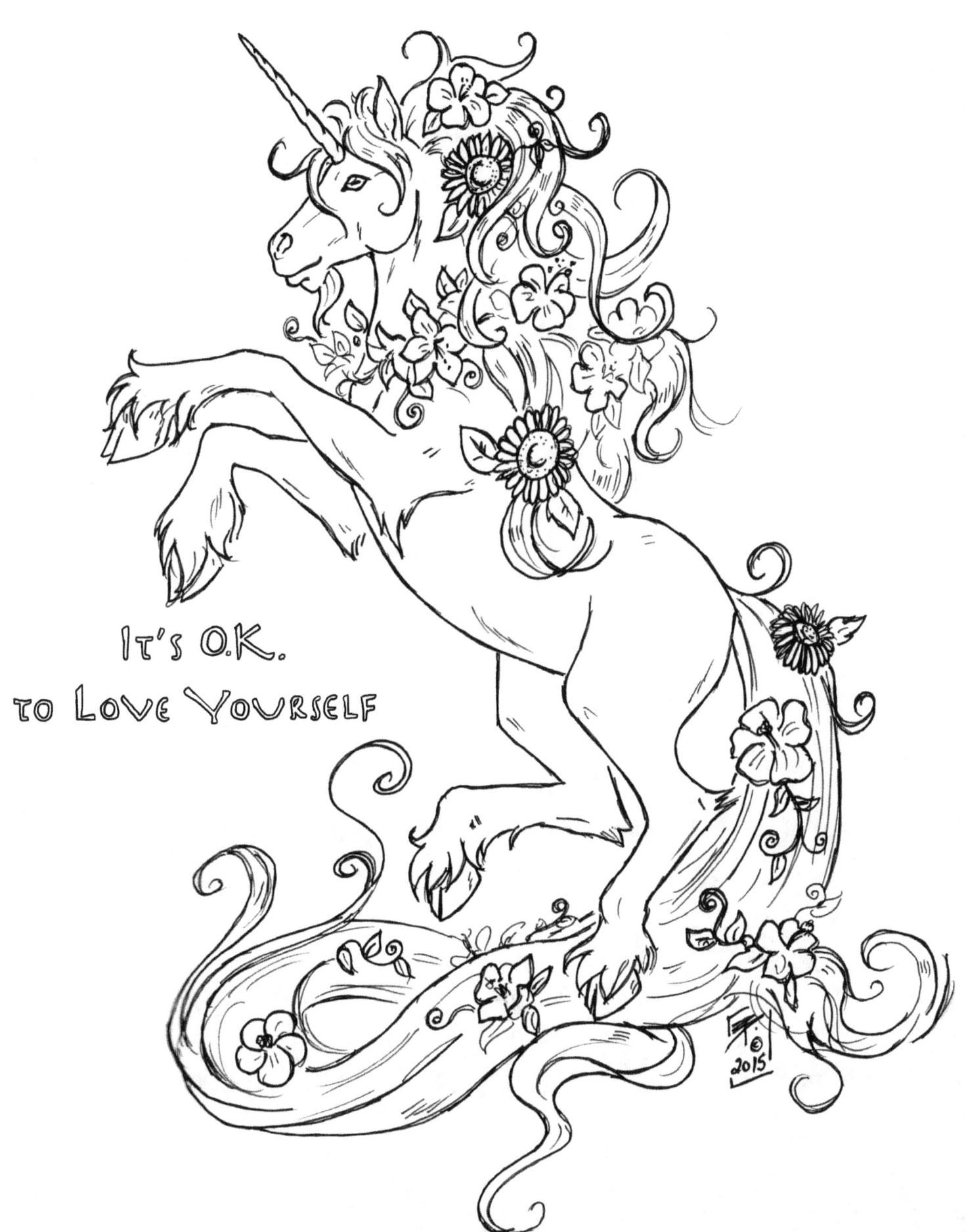

It's O.K.
to Love Yourself

"Hibiscus & Sunflower" © Brandy Woods 2015

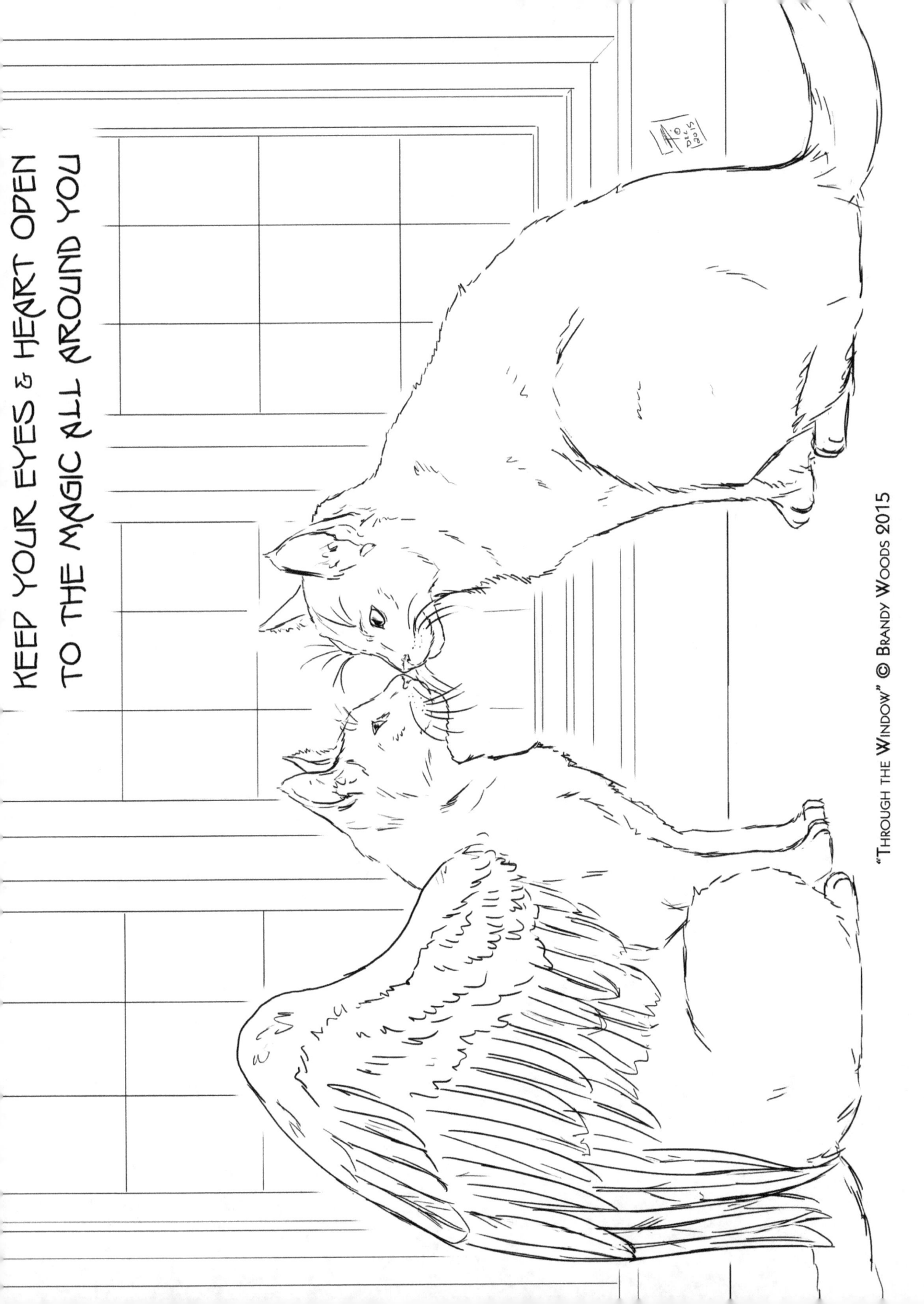

KEEP YOUR EYES & HEART OPEN
TO THE MAGIC ALL AROUND YOU

"THROUGH THE WINDOW" © BRANDY WOODS 2015

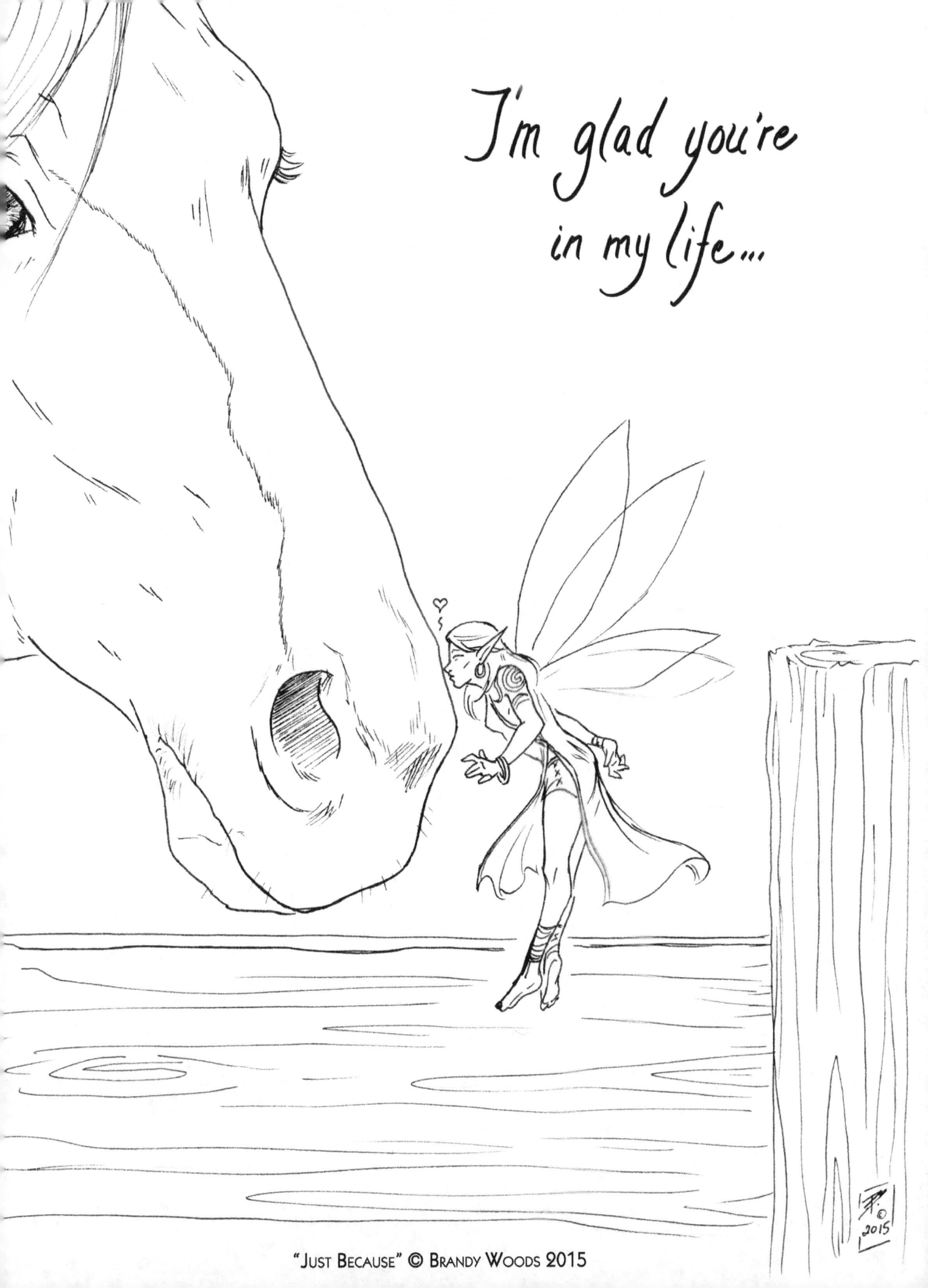

I'm glad you're in my life...

"JUST BECAUSE" © BRANDY WOODS 2015

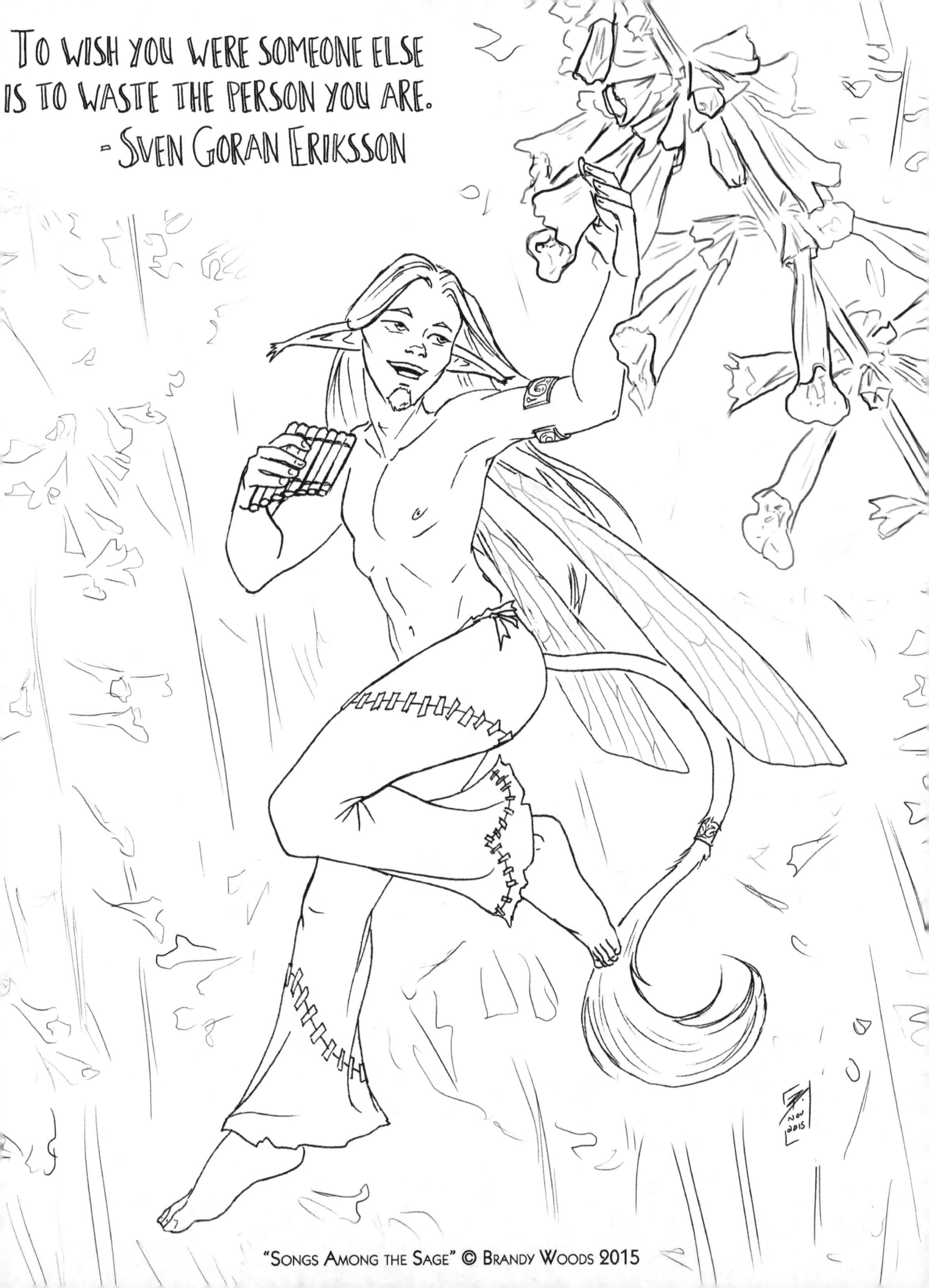

To wish you were someone else is to waste the person you are.
- Sven Goran Eriksson

"Songs Among the Sage" © Brandy Woods 2015

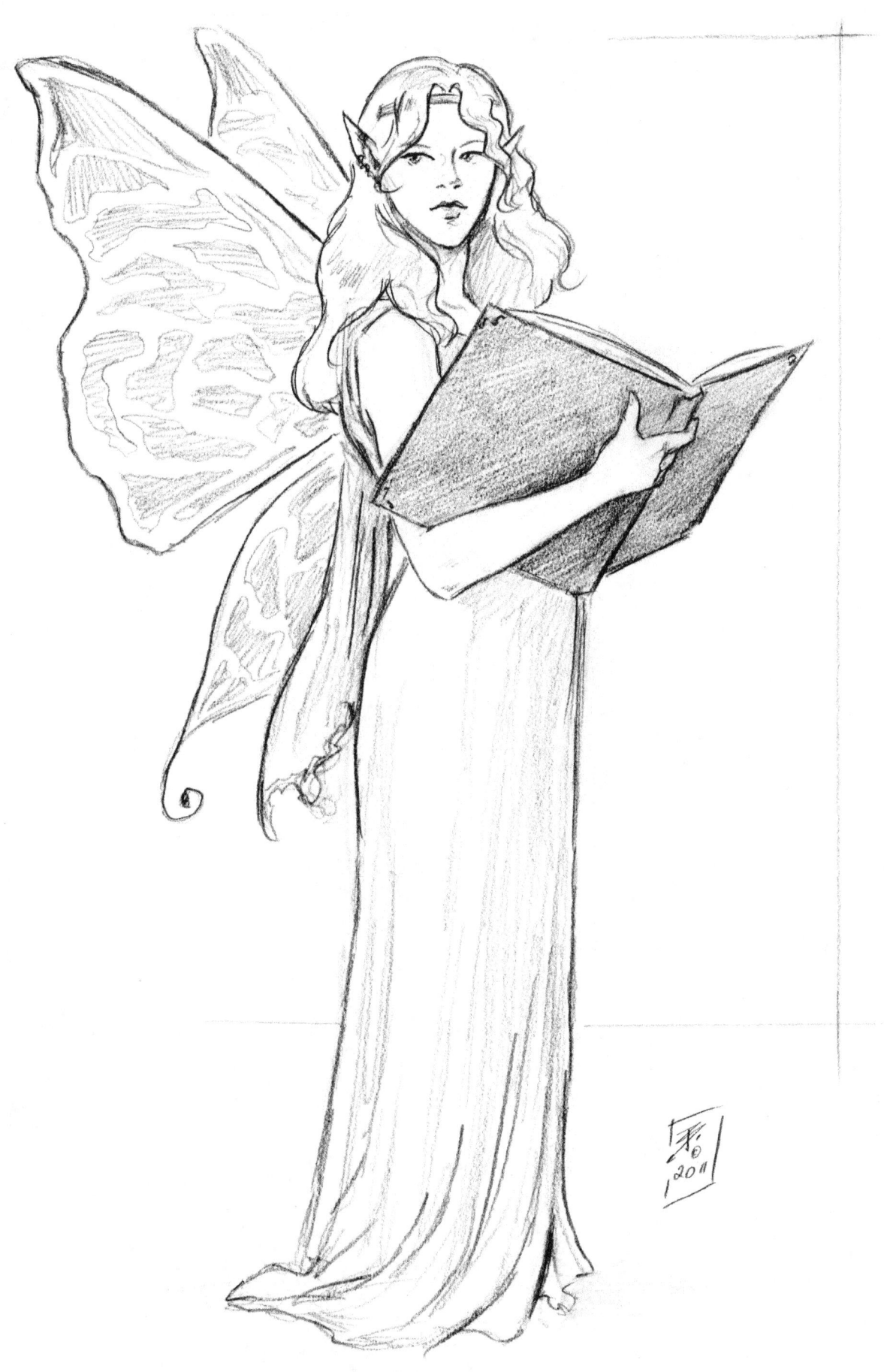

"Fairy Wisdom" © Brandy Woods 2011

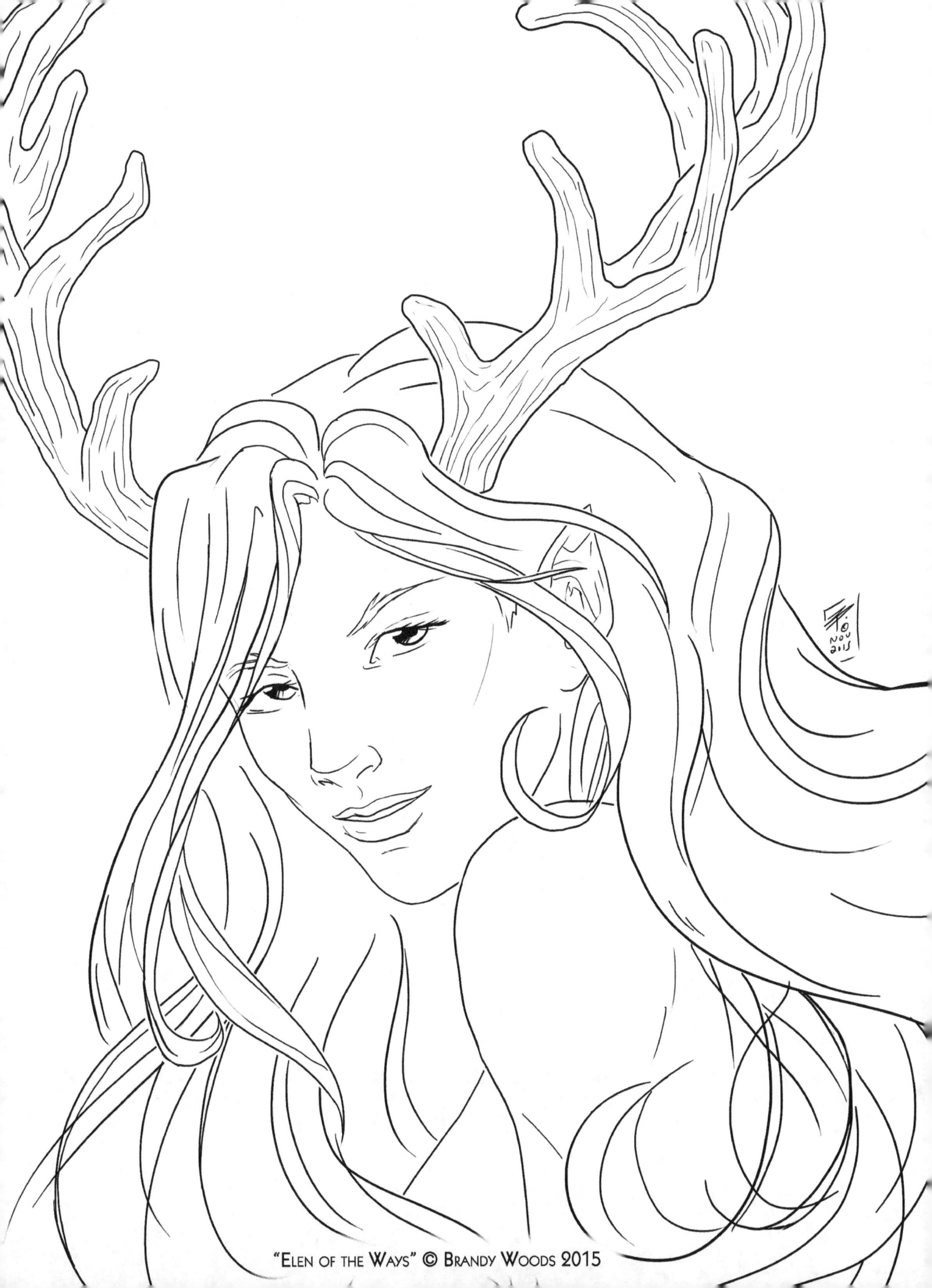

"Elen of the Ways" © Brandy Woods 2015

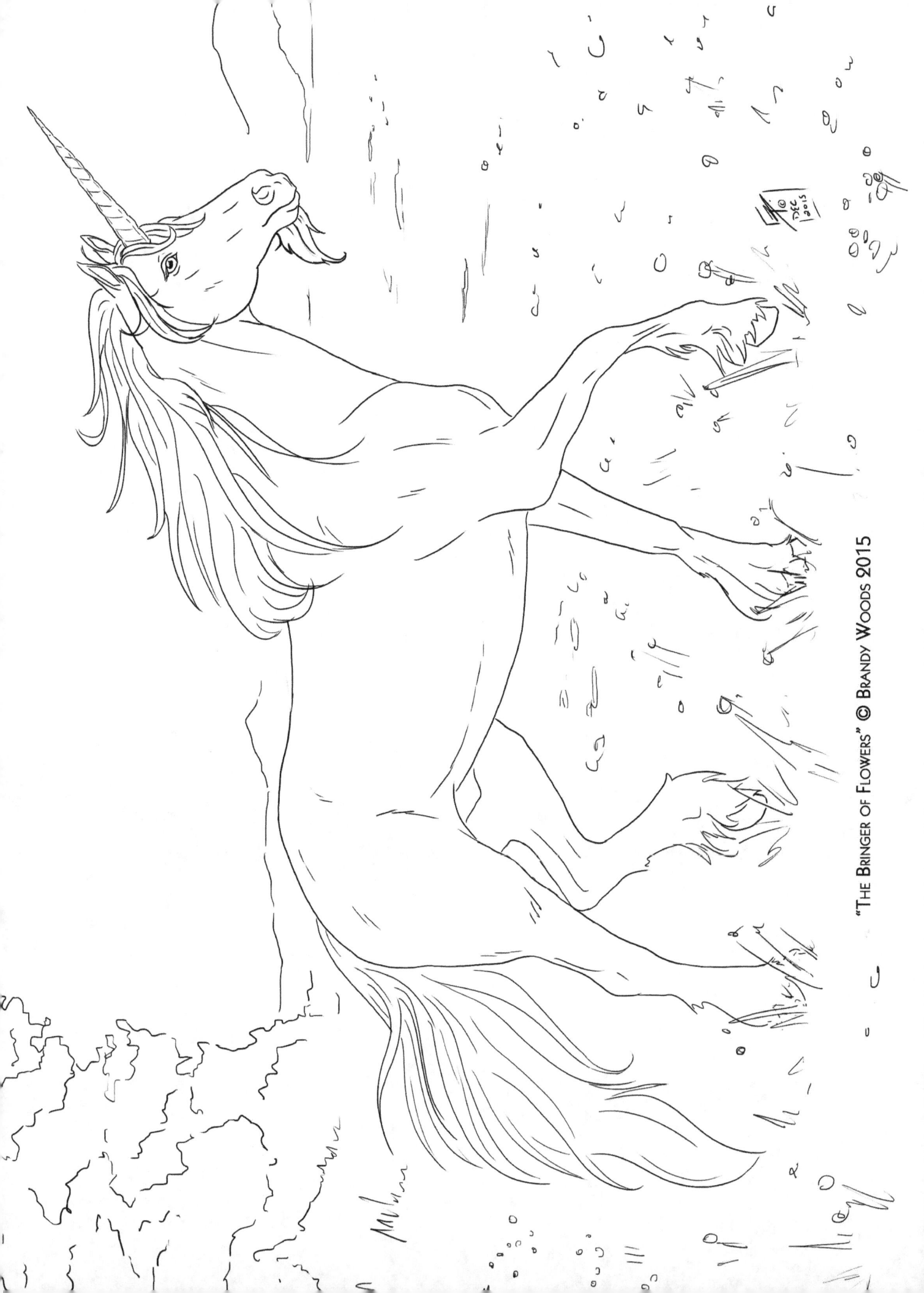

"The Bringer of Flowers" © Brandy Woods 2015

LIFE IS MORE FUN WITH FRIENDS WHO HELP YOU SOAR TO NEW HEIGHTS!

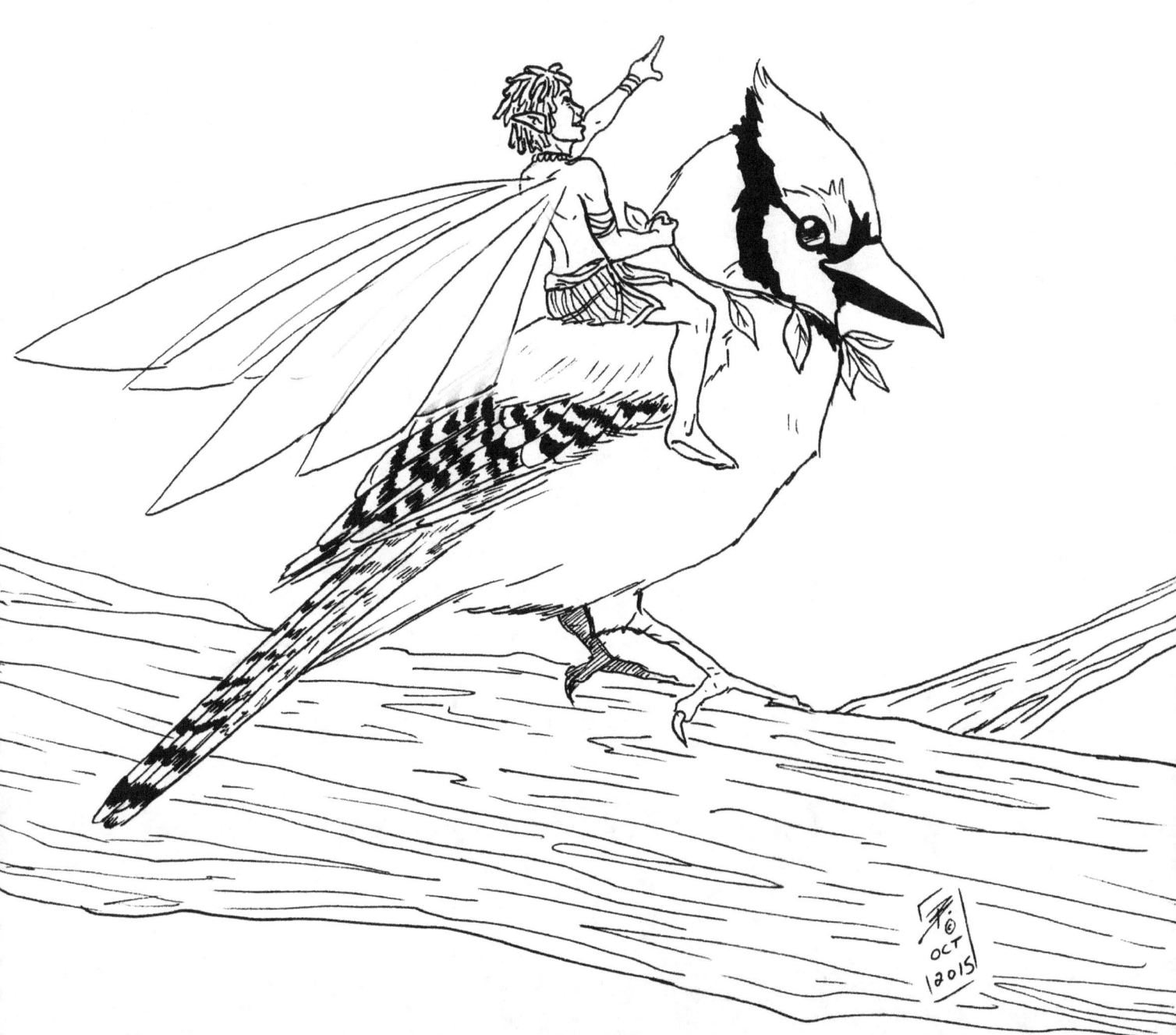

"Let's Fly!" © Brandy Woods 2015

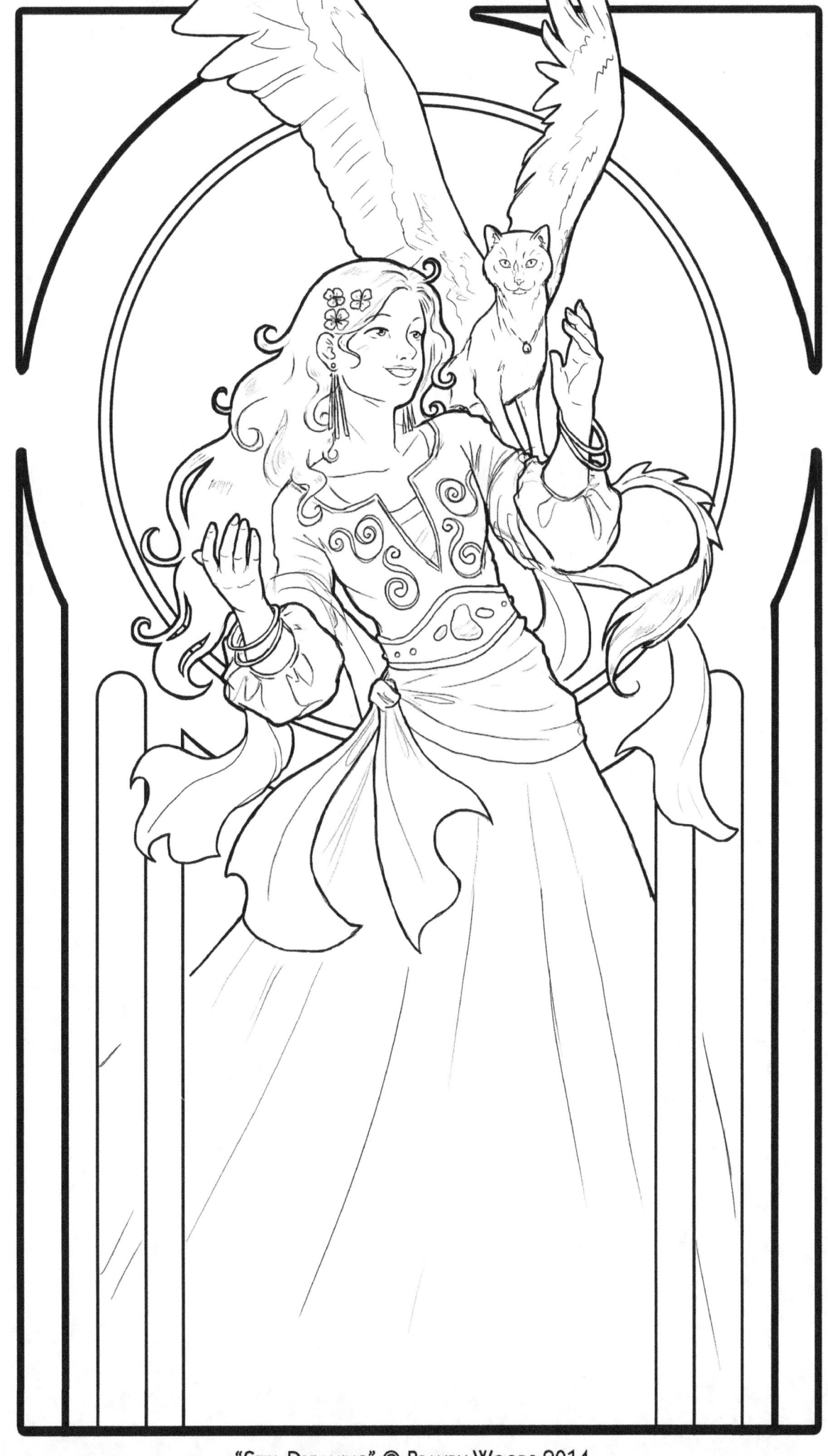

"STILL DREAMING" © BRANDY WOODS 2014

Spread Your Wings

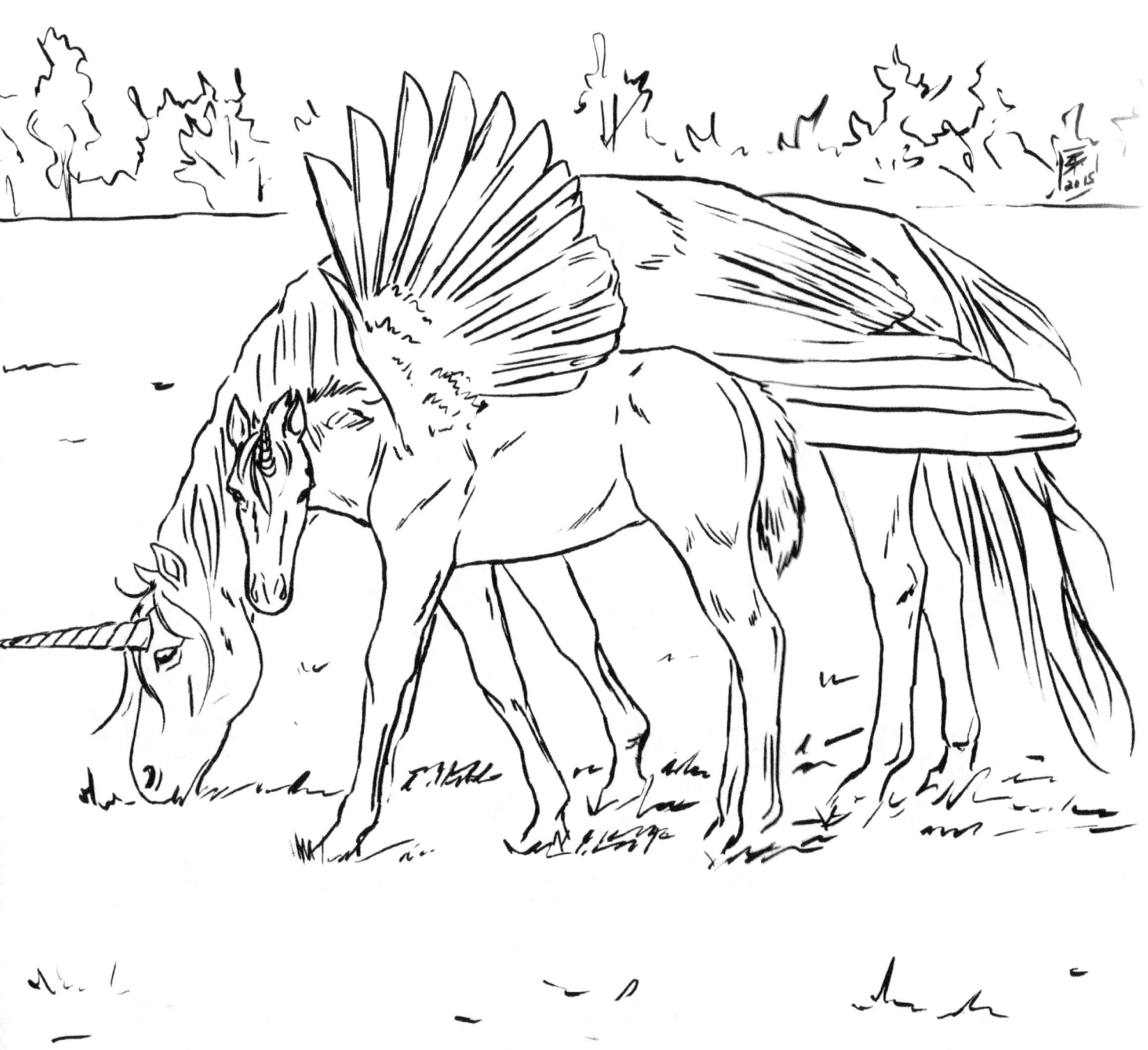

"The Newborn" © Brandy Woods 2015

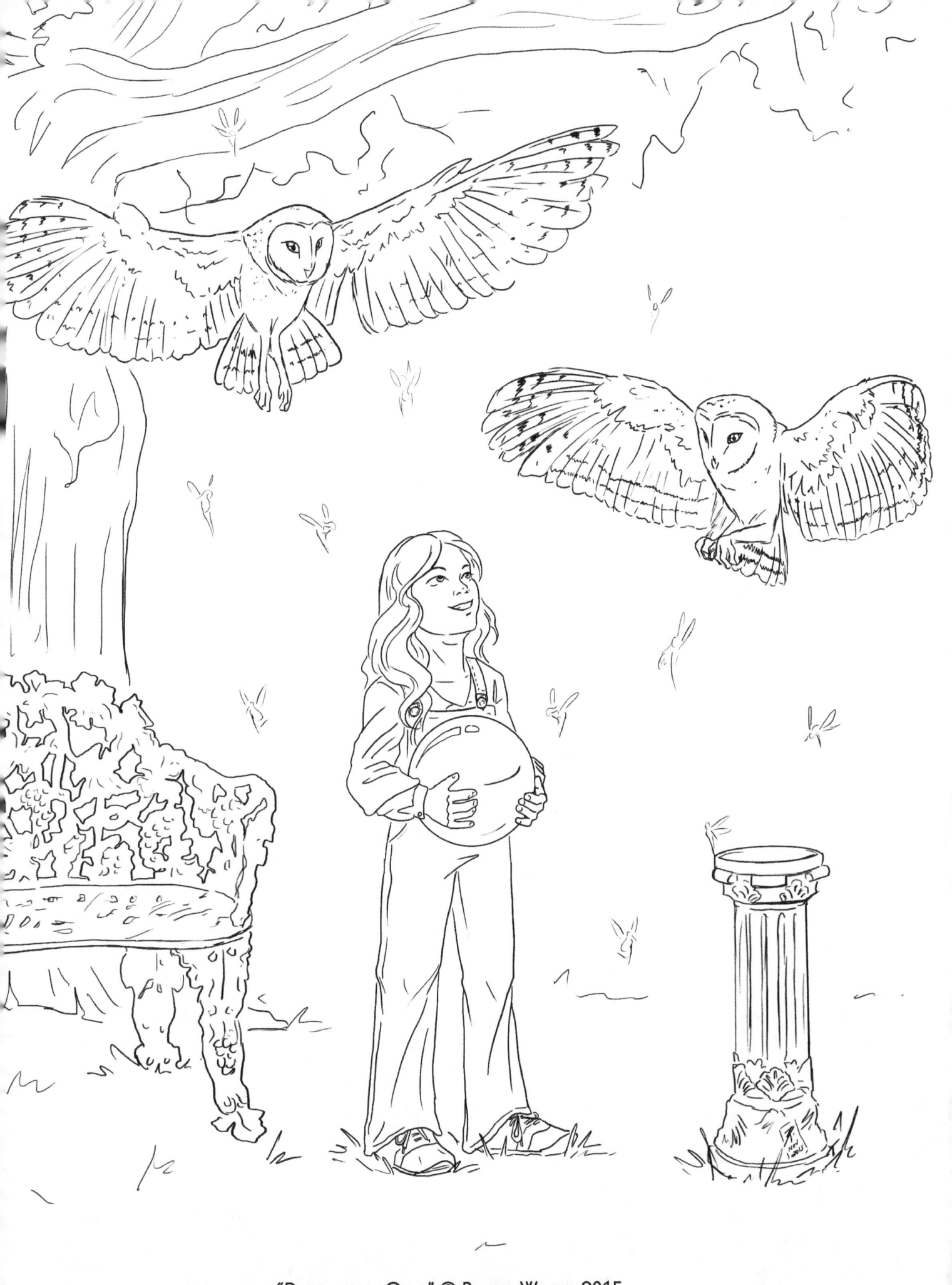

"Daughter of Owls" © Brandy Woods 2015

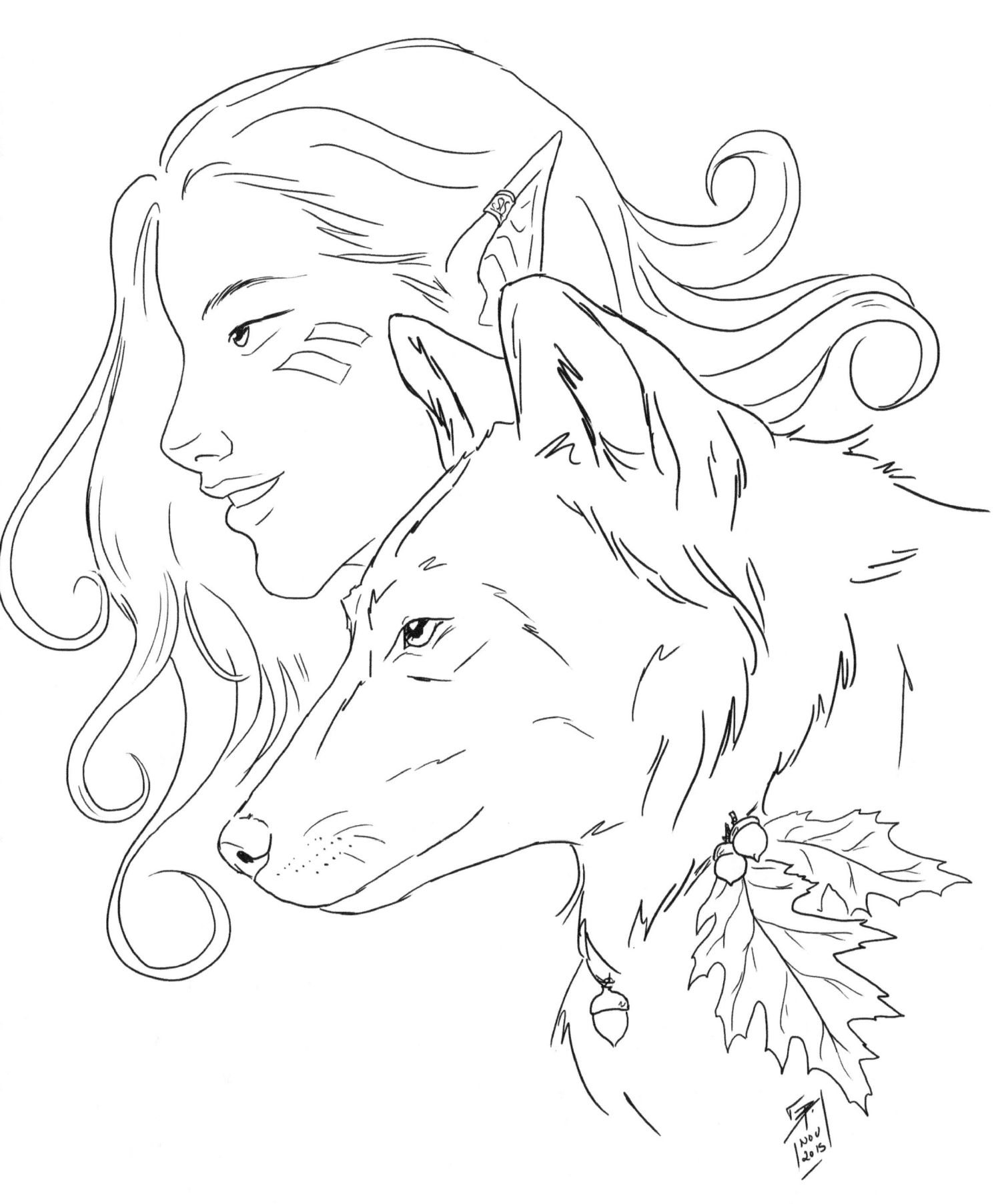

"Wolf Friend" © Brandy Woods 2015

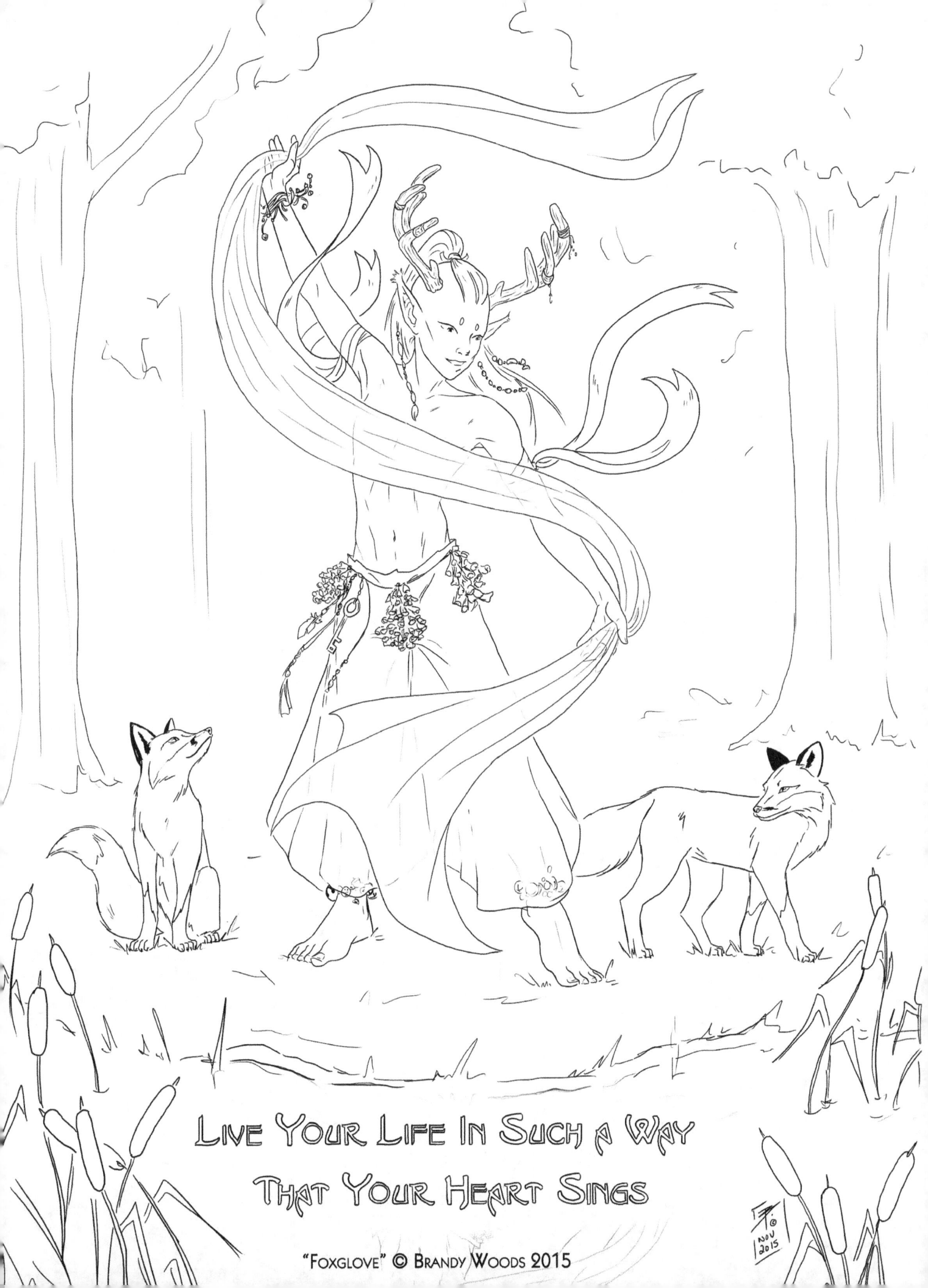

LIVE YOUR LIFE IN SUCH A WAY
THAT YOUR HEART SINGS

"Foxglove" © Brandy Woods 2015

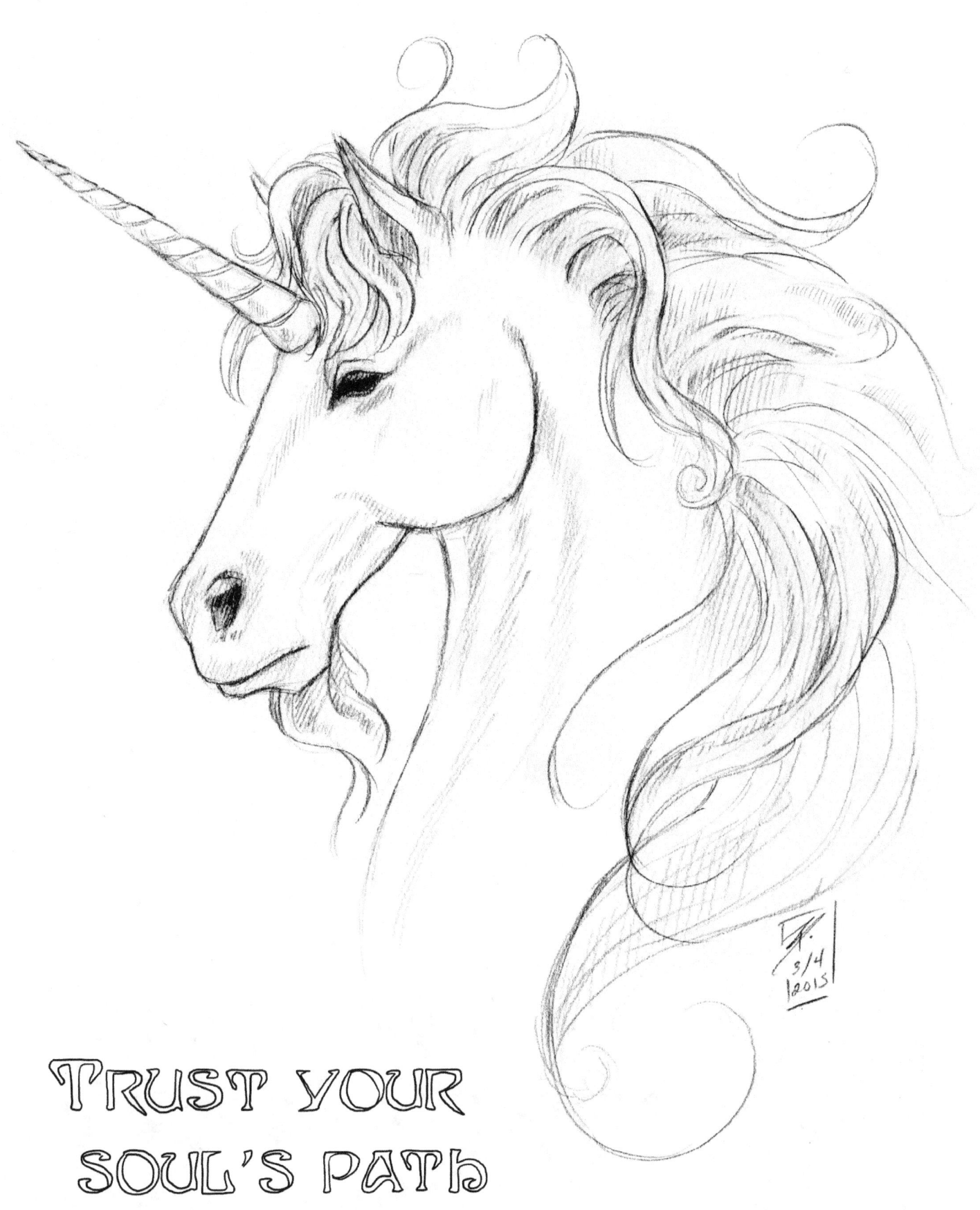

TRUST YOUR
SOUL'S PATH

"Unicorn Portrait" © Brandy Woods 2015

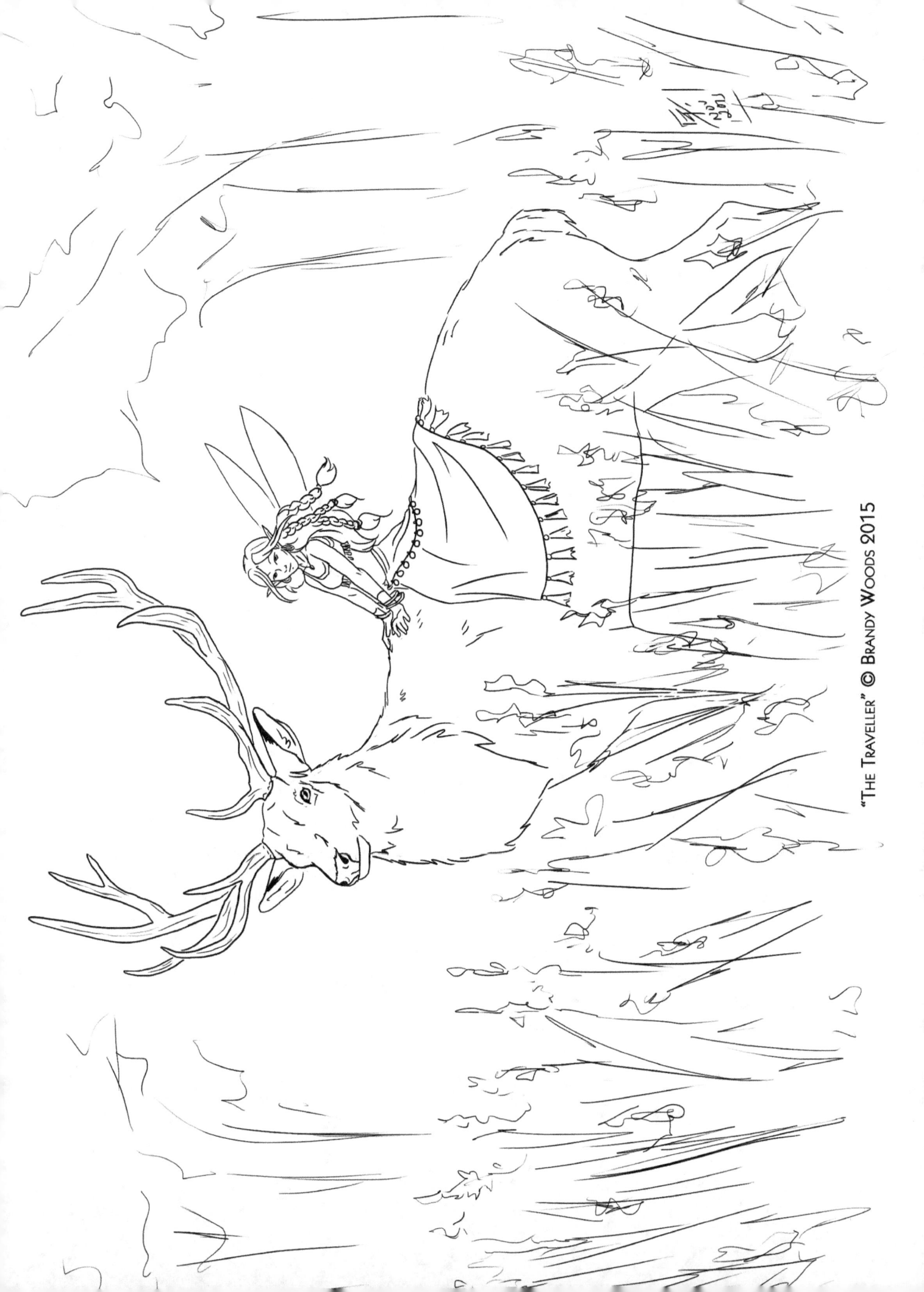

"The Traveller" © Brandy Woods 2015

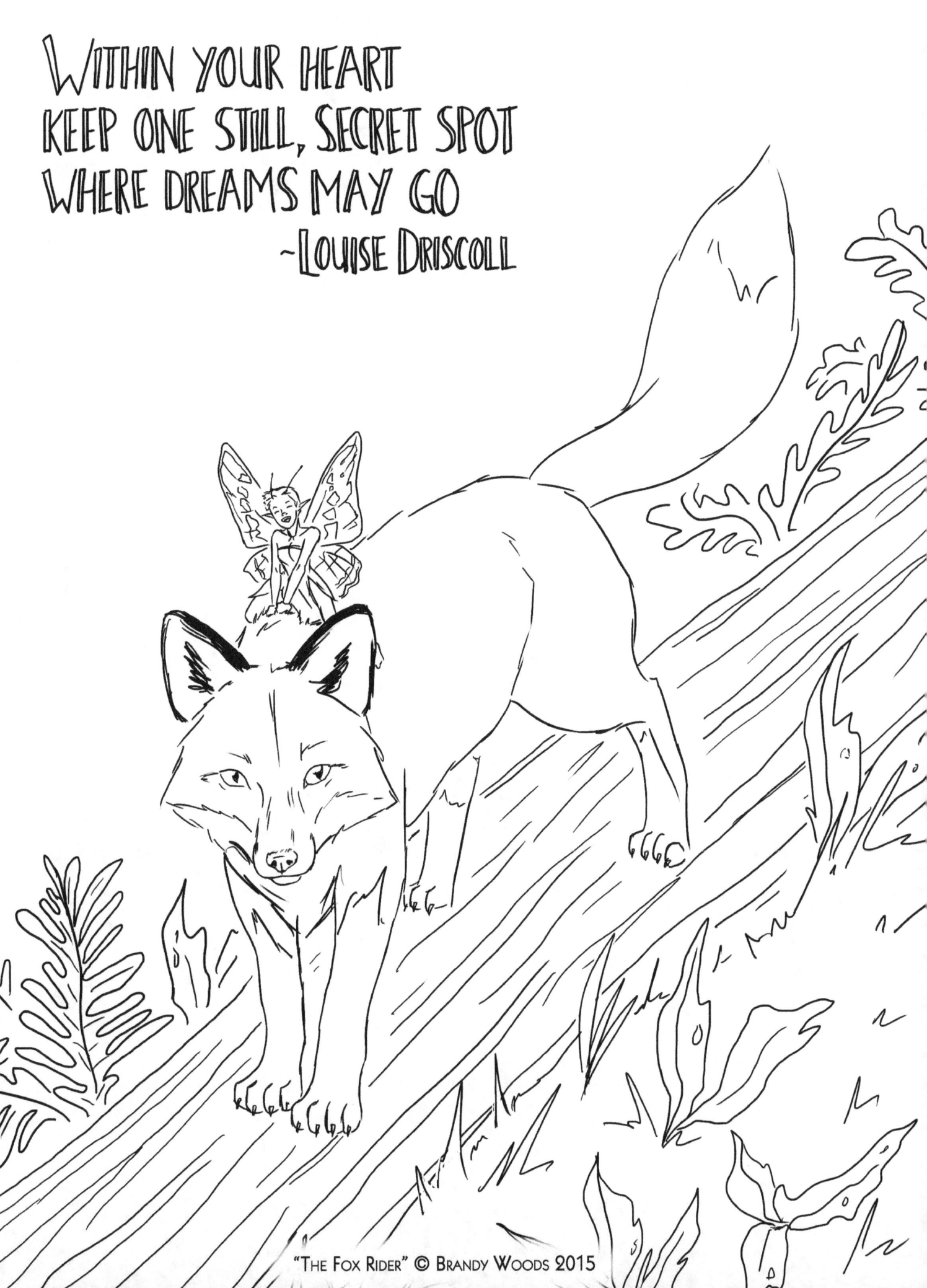

WITHIN YOUR HEART
KEEP ONE STILL, SECRET SPOT
WHERE DREAMS MAY GO
~LOUISE DRISCOLL

"THE FOX RIDER" © BRANDY WOODS 2015

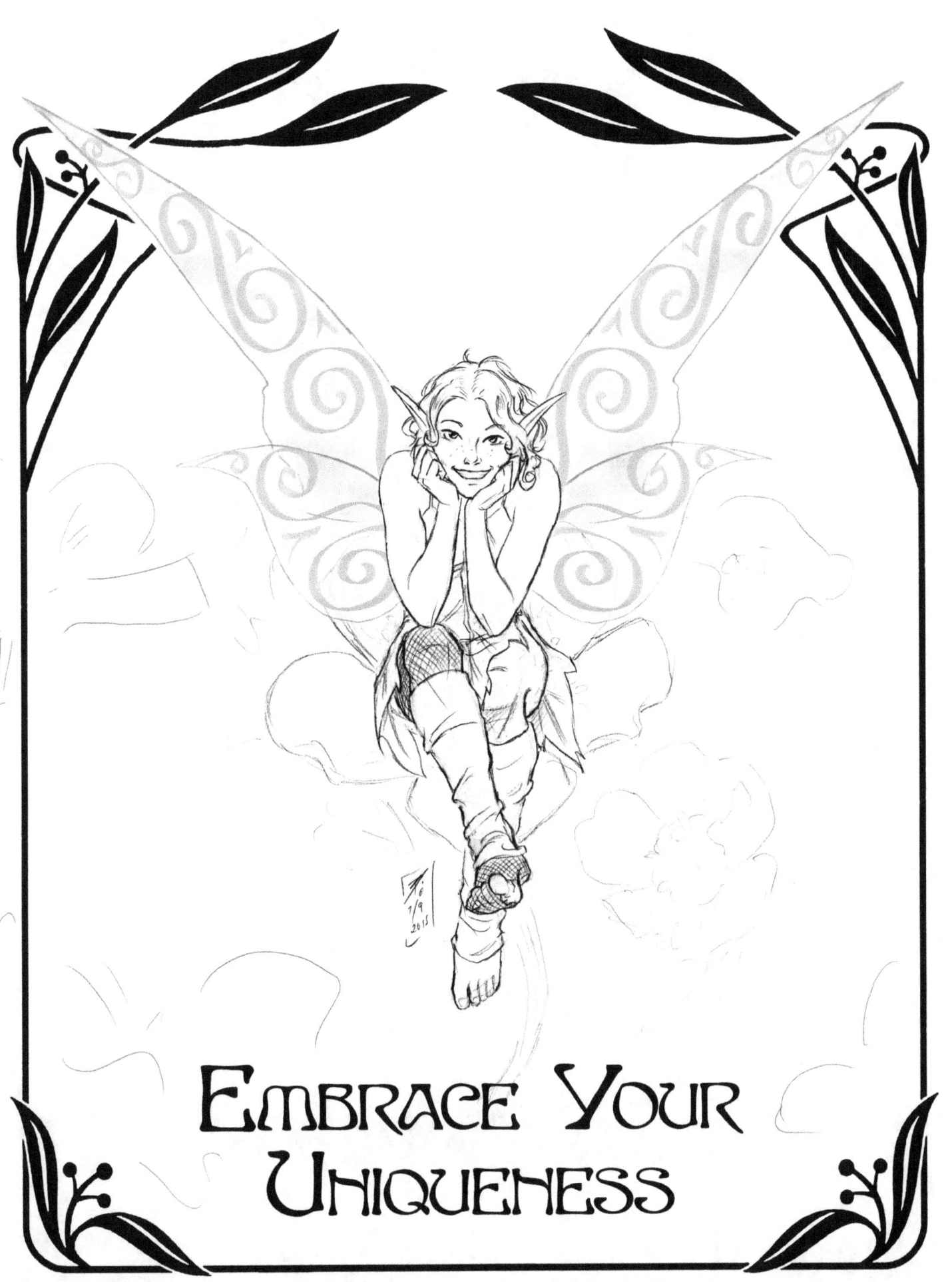

Embrace Your Uniqueness

"Buttercup" © Brandy Woods 2015

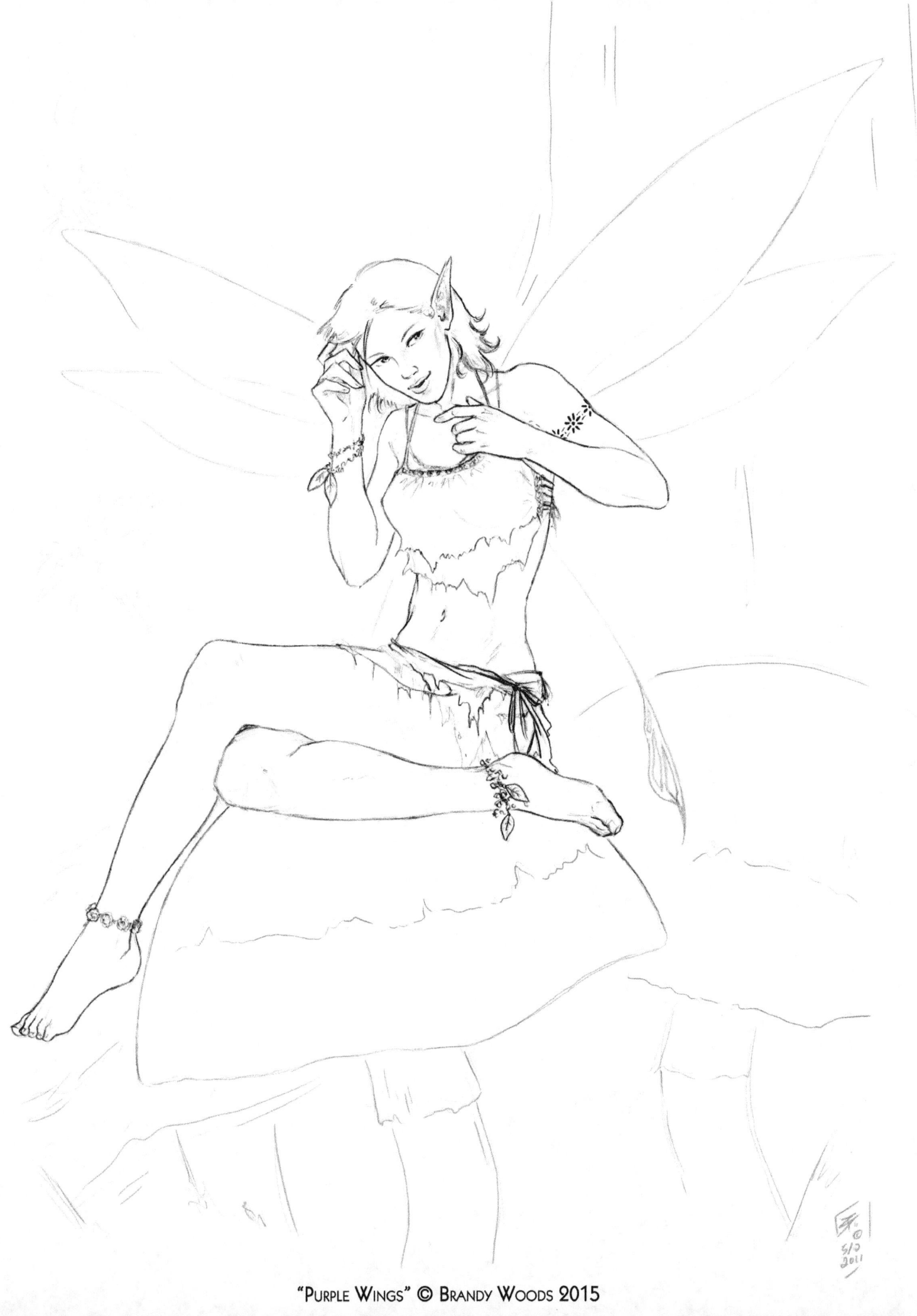

"Purple Wings" © Brandy Woods 2015

IT'S IMPORTANT
TO STAND UP FOR YOURSELF

"The Hat Thief" © Brandy Woods 2015

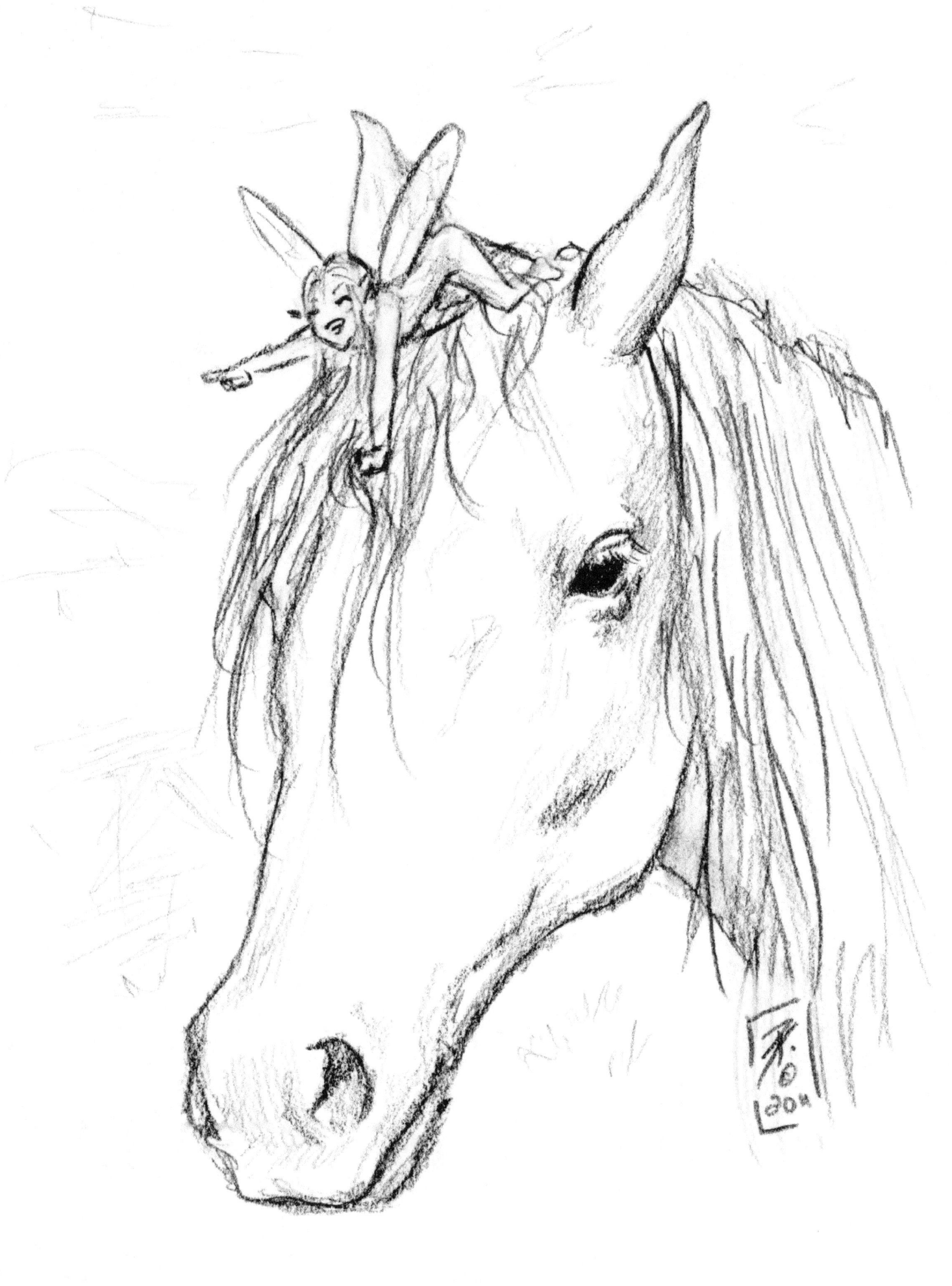

"Giddy Up" © Brandy Woods 2011

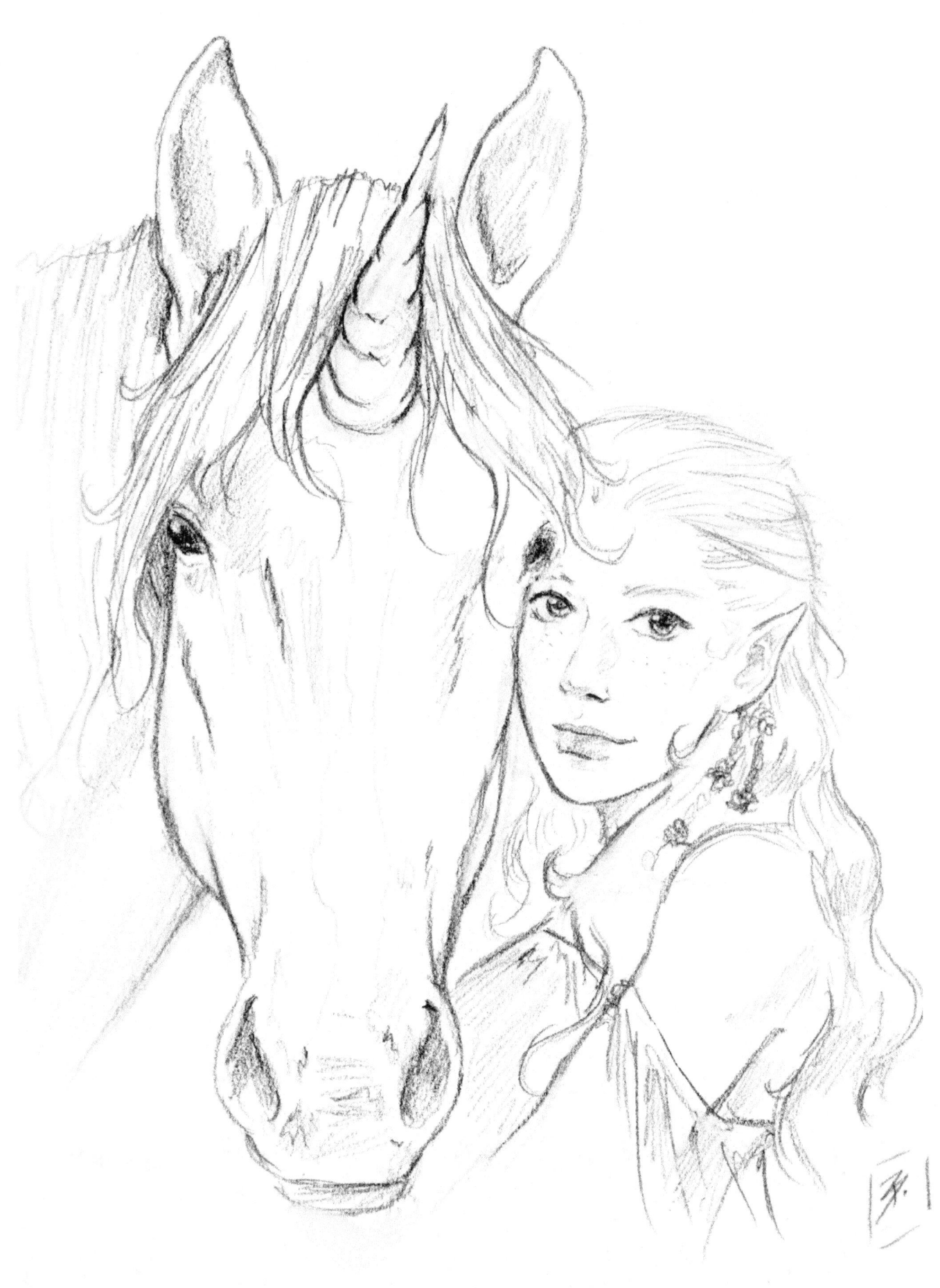

"Gentle" © Brandy Woods 2011

I would like to thank everyone who pledged
on Kickstarter to help bring this project to life!

You're all wonderful!

~
A Sutton fan
Anne Roisin
Becky & Darrell Woods
Brianne Goetz
C. M. Long
Cindy Perno
Darlene Maier
Delphine Lévesque Demers
Elizabeth Van Gulick
Gabe Velarde
J. Matusiak
John Austin
Jon Dailey
Junebug
Kelsey Blake
Koen Vingerhoets
Macia Davidson
Marie-Hélène Boivin
Marshmellow
Milissa Mumfrey
Papazark
Sophie Duvieusart
Steve Thomson
Yann Brouillette
~

www.ingramcontent.com/pod-product-compliance
Lightning Source LLC
Chambersburg PA
CBHW080841170526

45158CB00009B/2603